Hello, Family Members,

Learning to read is one of the most important accomplishments of early childhood. **Hello Reader!** books are designed to help children become skilled readers who like to read. Beginning readers learn to read by remembering frequently used words like "the," "is," and "and"; by using phonics skills to decode new words; and by interpreting picture and text clues. These books provide both the stories children enjoy and the structure they need to read fluently and independently. Here are suggestions for helping your child *before*, *during*, and *after* reading:

Before
- Look at the cover and pictures and have your child predict what the story is about.
- Read the story to your child.
- Encourage your child to chime in with familiar words and phrases.
- Echo read with your child by reading a line first and having your child read it after you do.

During
- Have your child think about a word he or she does not recognize right away. Provide hints such as "Let's see if we know the sounds" and "Have we read other words like this one?"
- Encourage your child to use phonics skills to sound out new words.
- Provide the word for your child when more assistance is needed so that he or she does not struggle and the experience of reading with you is a positive one.
- Encourage your child to have fun by reading with a lot of expression . . . like an actor!

After
- Have your child keep lists of interesting and favorite words.
- Encourage your child to read the books over and over again. Have him or her read to brothers, sisters, grandparents, and even teddy bears. Repeated readings develop confidence in young readers.
- Talk about the stories. Ask and answer questions. Share ideas about the funniest and most interesting characters and events in the stories.

I do hope that you and your child enjoy this book.

—Francie Alexander
Chief Education Officer,
Scholastic's Learning Ventures

With a magma-tude of thanks
to Stan Williams, John Ewert,
and Jackie Chua
— L.J.H.

ISBN 0-439-20544-1

Text copyright © 2001 by Lorraine Jean Hopping.
Illustrations copyright © 2001 by Jody Wheeler.
All rights reserved. Published by Scholastic Inc.
SCHOLASTIC, HELLO READER, CARTWHEEL BOOKS, and associated logos are trademarks and/or registered trademarks of Scholastic Inc.

Library of Congress Cataloging-in-Publication Data
Hopping, Lorraine Jean.
    Wild earth : volcano! / by Lorraine Jean Hopping ; illustrated by Jody Wheeler.
        p.   cm.—(Hello reader! Science—Level 4)
    ISBN 0-439-20544-1 (pbk)
        1. Volcanoes—Juvenile literature. [1. Volcanoes.] I. Title: Volcano!.
    II. Wheeler, Jody, ill. III. Title IV. Series.

QE521.3 .H67 2001
551.21—dc21   00-058380

12   11   10   9   8   7   6   5   4   3   2   1   01   02   03   04   05   06

Printed in the U.S.A.   24
First printing, October 2001

Volcano!

by Lorraine Jean Hopping
Illustrated by Jody Wheeler

Hello Reader! Science — Level 4

SCHOLASTIC INC. · Cartwheel B·O·O·K·S ·®

New York   Toronto   London   Auckland   Sydney
Mexico City   New Delhi   Hong Kong

Chapter 1

We Live on a Volcano

The whole village, 20 or so people, watched the stranger in silence.

For weeks, their mountain home had been acting strangely.
Starting in April of 1991, Mount Pinatubo [PEE-nah-TOO-boe] burped up hot gases.
It spit out rocks like watermelon seeds.

In May, the mountain sometimes shook and rumbled with a terrible noise.
Clouds of ash and steam shot up through cracks in the ground.

To the surprise of the villagers, they were living on top of a volcano!

The villagers were Aetas [EYE-tahs], a mountain people of the Philippines, an island nation in Asia.

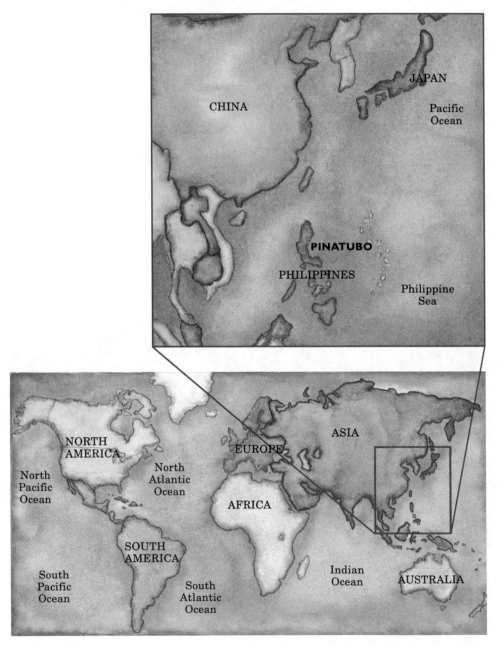

The strangers were scientists.
They rushed to set up instruments
that measure earthquakes, one sign
of a coming explosion.

The Aeta village of Patal Pinto was
near the volcano's vent, a mile-long
crack in the ground.
John Ewert, an American scientist,
felt uneasy working near the heart
of the volcano.
What about the people who *lived*
there?
"We didn't speak their language,"
John said. "No one had told them
how dangerous the volcano was."

The scientists found someone to
warn the Aetas.
He said, "If you feel lots of
earthquakes or hear strange, loud
noises, *leave* immediately!"

From the air, Pinatubo didn't look dangerous.

"It was just a dome, nothing special," John said. "But the land all around the dome was very scary."

The land showed that Pinatubo had blown up many times, long ago. Those blasts were awesome. The volcano had tossed a blanket of ash, rocks, and lava as far as John could see. Hot mudflows called lahars [LAH-harz] had carved gullies into the blanket like giant plows in a cornfield.

"Only nature has the power to change the earth like that," John said.

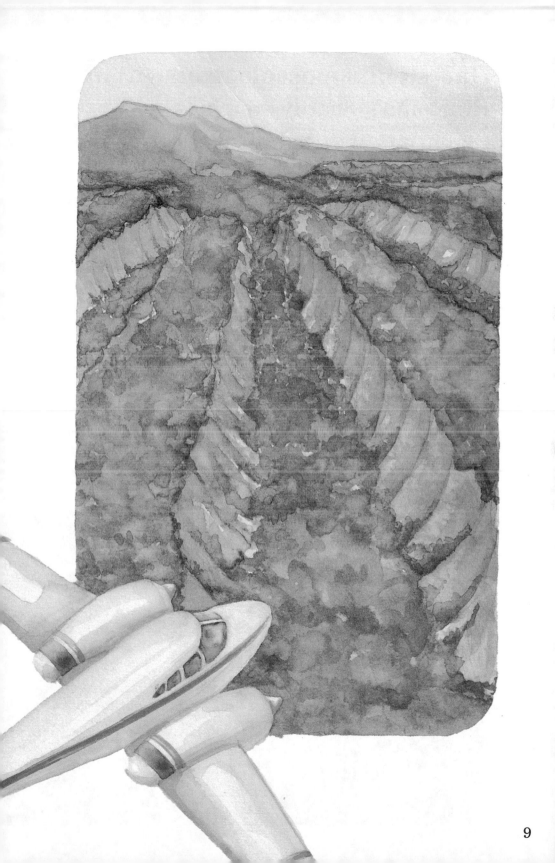

Half a million people lived within Pinatubo's deadly reach.
Scientists warned officials to move everyone away from the volcano.

People could only take what they could carry.
What should they bring?
What would they have to leave behind?

Families left their houses, crops, farm animals, and other items.
They lived for days in hot, crowded shelters.
They ate. They slept. They waited.
But nothing happened.
The volcano did not blow up.

The scientists were still sure that Pinatubo would erupt.
They just didn't know when.

The scientists studied Pinatubo from a nearby air force base called Clark.
Like the Aetas, workers at Clark had not known Pinatubo was a volcano.

Soon, the whole world knew.

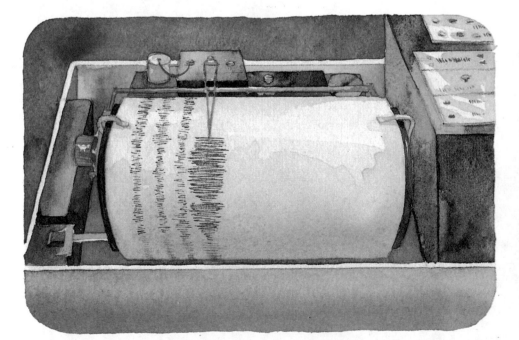

Chapter 2

Earthquakes, Floods, and a Typhoon, Too

The instruments on Pinatubo collected plenty of earthquake data. Radios sent the data to Clark Air Base in a nonstop stream.

Scientist Perla De Los Reyes read the data closely.
The data showed hundreds of earthquakes beneath the mountain. And the quakes were getting bigger.

Scientists warned officials to keep people away from the volcano.

The scientists were worried.
What if the volcano didn't erupt
after they told people that it would?

People might go back home.
They might not listen to anymore
warnings to go to safety.

But the volcano *did* erupt.
On June 12, 1991, it blew a cloud of
ash many miles high.
The sky turned as dark as night.

Hot ash fell everywhere like a dirty, gritty snowfall.
Children covered their mouths with cloth and their heads with pots.

Yet this blast was a small one.

"The volcano was just clearing its throat," John Ewert explained. "It was getting ready for the big one."

Meanwhile, a typhoon [tye-FOON], or hurricane, was about to hit the area. The scientists were stunned. A typhoon and a volcano at the same time? Unbelievable!

In the early morning of June 15, the scientists at Clark fled to safety. But a few hours later, they returned.

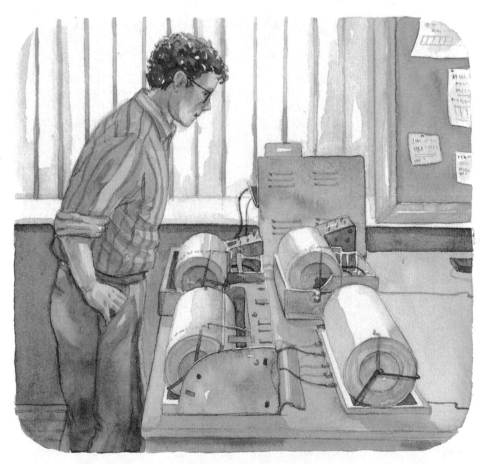

"No one was there to look at the earthquake data," John explained. The scientists needed that data in order to tell people what Pinatubo was doing.

A few hours later, all the data stopped coming in.
Something had wrecked the instruments.
It was Pinatubo! The volcano was exploding, big time!

The scientists left the base again,
one step ahead of the volcano.

Rain from the typhoon caused
wet ash and small volcanic rocks
to fall from the sky.
The gray ash buried towns
and farms.
It caved in roofs at Clark.

"We should not have stayed so long,"
John said later. "Pinatubo
could have buried the base."

John doesn't know if the Aetas
of Patal Pinto left in time.
Their village no longer exists.

For years after the blast, lahars
destroyed homes and farmland.
These hot mudflows killed people,
farm animals, and wildlife.

In all, nearly a thousand people died.
But tens of thousands lived.
They lived because scientists risked
their lives to warn people that
a volcano was about to explode.

Chapter 3

Domes, Cones, and a Cornfield

A blast as big as Pinatubo might happen twice in your lifetime. Small eruptions happen about once a week on average.

The world's thousands of volcanoes spend most of their time asleep. Volcanoes can stay dormant for hundreds of years.

The Santa María volcano in Central
America slept for 2,000 years.
People thought it was extinct.
Extinct volcanoes are dead.
They are not supposed to blow up.

Yet in 1902, Santa María erupted.
Its blast was as big as Pinatubo's.

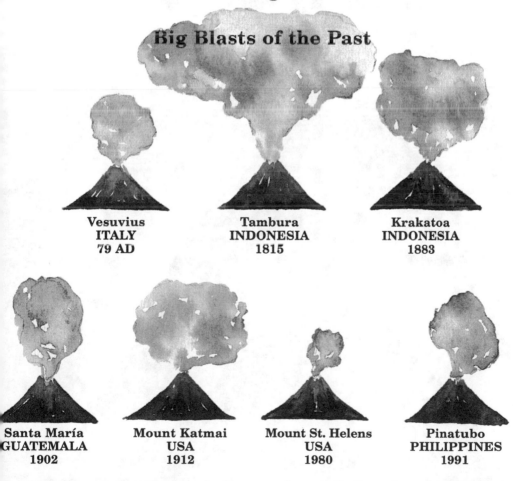

Big Blasts of the Past

Vesuvius
ITALY
79 AD

Tambura
INDONESIA
1815

Krakatoa
INDONESIA
1883

Santa María
GUATEMALA
1902

Mount Katmai
USA
1912

Mount St. Helens
USA
1980

Pinatubo
PHILIPPINES
1991

Relative sizes of blasts indicate volume of ejected materials.

Inside a Volcano

ash

lava rock

crust

vents

magma

Volcanoes form over cracks in the Earth's crust called vents.
The crust is the ground you walk on.

Scientist Stan Williams calls volcano vents "windows that let us look inside the Earth."
The windows reveal a sea of super-hot, melted rock beneath the crust.
The liquid rock is called magma.

In an eruption, magma and gases shoot up through the vents.
A powerful blast can shatter magma into powdery ash.
Magma can also ooze out slowly.

Above ground, magma is called lava.
When lava cools and hardens into solid rock, it becomes part of the crust.

Most volcanoes have formed in a circle around the Pacific Ocean. (See map.)
Pinatubo and Santa María are part of this "Ring of Fire."

Tens of thousands of volcanoes are on the ocean floor. They erupt deep under the water.
Each eruption adds a layer of lava. The volcano grows a little taller.

Volcanoes of the World

ASIA

Mount Pinatub

Indian Ocean

AUSTRALIA

Some undersea volcanoes grow tall
enough to rise above the surface of
the water.
Their tips form islands, such as the
Hawaiian Islands.

Ring of
Fire

Mount
St. Helens

NORTH
AMERICA

Hawaiian
Islands

Mount
Pelée

Atlantic
Ocean

Santa
María

Nevado del
Ruiz

Galeras

SOUTH
AMERICA

South Pacific
Ocean

Picture a volcano in your mind.
Does it look like an upside down
ice-cream cone with a pointy tip?

Many volcanoes look that way.
Mount St. Helens, in the state of
Washington, once did.
The cone volcano even had "icing,"
sparkly white snow on top!

Then on May 18, 1980, the volcano
blew itself apart.

A big chunk blasted away from the
side of the volcano.

Afterward, Mount St. Helens looked
like a molar tooth with a cavity.

Some volcanoes look like
upside down bowls.
They are called shield volcanoes.

Olympus Mons on the planet Mars
is one giant example.
This mountain is the biggest known
volcano in the solar system.

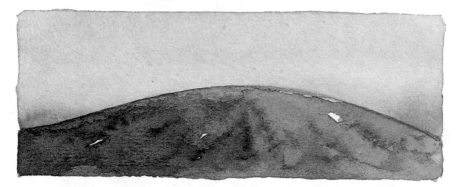

Olympus Mons, a shield volcano

Mount St. Helens, a cone volcano

One volcano in California is a valley,
not a mountain.
In fact, it is called Long Valley.
Long ago, the volcano blasted itself
to bits in a huge eruption.
The valley is all that's left.
It is actually a crater called a caldera
[kal-DARE-ah].

A new caldera formed in Pinatubo,
at the site of its 1991 explosion.
The caldera filled with water and
formed a lake.

Mount Pinatubo, caldera and lake

In 1943, a volcano erupted in the middle of a cornfield in Mexico!

Lava popped out of a hole in the ground on and off for ten years. It landed all around the vent. Layer by layer, the lava formed a small cone.

Chapter 4

A Million Lives

What makes volcanoes explode?

"Gas!" said Stan Williams, a volcano scientist.

Gases are trapped in magma like bubbles in a capped soda bottle.

Stan explained, "When you take off the cap, bubbles form and the soda flies all over, getting you in trouble."

Gases trapped in magma do the same thing.
Their "cap" is a layer of crust over the vents.

Magma moves around under the crust, causing earthquakes.

When the moving magma "pops the cap," gases burst out in an explosion.

Before a blast, some gas rises through the rocks.
Scientists can collect and measure that gas.
The amount and type of gas can help them predict an eruption.

For example, both Pinatubo and Mount St. Helens were full of trapped steam.
Steam is water in the form of gas.

Open a bottle cap a tiny bit.
Gas hisses out slowly, and the soda
doesn't explode.

"If a vent is not tightly sealed, gases
are released over time," Stan said.
"So the magma can't explode."

One volcano in Africa is very leaky.
Its vent is on the bottom of a lake
called Nyos [NEE-ohs].

In 1986, the Lake Nyos volcano
burped up a cloud of carbon dioxide.
The gas bubbled out of the lake.
It spread over the land, killing 1,700
people and their farm animals.

One little burp of gas killed more
people than Pinatubo did!

Like the Lake Nyos volcano,
Kilauea [kil-ah-WAY-ah] in Hawaii
doesn't explode.
One reason is that its magma
is thin, just as water is thinner
than honey.
Gas bubbles easily rise out
of the thin magma and escape.

By the time the volcano erupts, the
magma has little gas left.

It is like flat soda pop.
The magma oozes out slowly or
spurts out in red fountains.

The super-hot liquid destroys roads,
towns, and plant life in its path.
Fortunately, people usually have
time to get out of the way.

Gas explosions, even small ones, are far more dangerous than lava.

In 1993, Stan and his team climbed Galeras [gah-LARE-ahs], a volcano in South America. The scientists wanted to study some odd, yellow rocks. The tiny rocks were spread around like icing on a cake.

"I am often very scared while I am working on volcanoes," Stan said. "You feel the earth shake. You hear rocks shake loose and fall down."

You also smell hot gases that have seeped up through the rocks.

On Galeras, a sudden blast of gas tossed boulders into the air. Rocks the size of TV sets rained down on the scientists.

Six scientists and three hikers died.
Stan had two broken legs, a broken
skull, and other injuries.
His friends carried him to safety.

One friend, Marta Lucia Calvache,
solved the mystery of the yellow
rocks.
They had piled up in the vents.
Gas explosions had thrown them
out.

Stan spent months getting well.
Then he went right back to work.

"If you work on volcanoes, you
must learn to accept very dangerous
events," Stan said. "But I did not
foresee that I must also learn how
to see the death of friends."

Why do volcano scientists risk their lives?
John Ewert gave two good reasons.

One reason is Nevado del Ruiz [neh-VAH-doe del roo-EES], a volcano in South America.
In 1985, a blast caused lahars, or mudflows, that killed 23,000 people.

The other reason is Mount Pelée [peh-LAY].
In 1902, the volcano killed 29,000 people on a Caribbean island.

"I want to help people learn to live with volcanoes," John said.

Stan agreed.
Some day, he predicted, a volcano could kill a million people.

"Your own life is not a big deal compared to a million lives," he said. "It might be worth it to take risks, if you can help people survive."

Chapter 5

Beautiful and Terrible

Volcanoes do kill people.
Yet we need volcanoes to live.
How can that be?

Air, for one thing.
The Earth's atmosphere is ma
of gases.
Volcanoes spew carbon dioxide
and other important gases into
our atmosphere.

Land is another gift.
The nation of Iceland is one of many
islands made by undersea volcanoes.

Volcanoes give us heat, too.
Iceland is in the Far North, where
temperatures are often cold.
People there pipe heat from
volcanoes into their homes.

Volcanoes even change our weather.
Pinatubo shot ash miles into the sky.
Wind blew the powder all the way
around the Earth.
The ash blocked out some of the
sun's rays, which cooled the planet.
In that way, volcanoes help keep the
Earth from getting too hot.

How else do volcanoes help us?

Their heat and gases help gold,
silver, and other minerals form.

Volcanic ash has nutrients that
help plants grow.
Many people live on volcanoes
in order to grow food crops.

John Ewert lives near volcanoes
for a different reason.
"I look out my window and can't
believe the beautiful view," he said.

Volcano Safety Tips

Stan Williams nearly lost his life on a volcano. If you travel on a volcano, follow his safety tips:

- Stay with a group. "I always travel with friends," says Stan. "We take care of each other."
- Wear bright colors so people can spot you easily.
- Take food, water, extra clothing, a flashlight, and a whistle. If you get lost or hurt, blow the whistle!

If a nearby volcano is acting up, listen to the radio or TV news. If officials tell you to leave, do it!